Media in Fragile Environments

MEDIA
in Fragile
Environments
The USIP Intended-Outcomes
Needs Assessment Methodology

Andrew Robertson
Eran Fraenkel
Emrys Schoemaker
Sheldon Himelfarb

United States Institute of Peace
Washington, D.C.

The views expressed in this guide are those of the author alone. They do not necessarily reflect views of the United States Institute of Peace.

United States Institute of Peace
2301 Constitution Ave., NW
Washington, DC 20037

Phone: 202-457-1700
Fax: 202-429-6063
E-mail: usip_requests@usip.org
Web: www.usip.org

First published 2011

To request permission to photocopy or reprint materials for course use, contact Copyright Clearance Center at www.copyright.com.

Printed in the United States of America

The paper used in this publication meets the minimum requirements of American National Standards for Information Science Permanence of Paper for Printed Library Materials, ANSI Z39.48-1984.

Library of Congress Cataloging-in-Publication Data

Media in fragile environments : the USIP intended-outcomes needs assessment methodology / Andrew Robertson ... [et al.].

    p. cm.

  ISBN 978-1-60127-081-8 (alk. paper)

1. Mass media and peace. 2. Mass media and peace—Developing countries. 3. United States Institute of Peace. 4. Peace-building—Developing countries. 5. Needs assessment—Developing countries. I. Robertson, Andrew W. (Andrew Whitmore), 1951-

P96.P33M44 2011

302.23—dc22

2011003095

Contents

Media in Fragile Environments: The USIP Intended-Outcomes Needs Assessment Methodology

The USIP Intended-Outcomes Needs Assessment (IONA) methodology enables NGOs, donors, and policymakers to determine which kinds of media interventions can most effectively address issues affecting a fragile society. Using a three-stage process, IONA enables an assessment team to analyze the causes of problems producing social fragility, interview members of that society to understand what changes are desirable and possible, and generate a portfolio of media programs that balance the needs of the society in conflict with the capabilities of that society's media. IONA can be used to understand the broad sweep of conflict-related issues in a society to determine an appropriate media intervention strategy. Alternatively, sponsors may wish to use IONA to better determine an appropriate media intervention strategy to address an issue or campaign that they have already identified, such as corruption, ethnic tension, or gender violence, to name just a few. Finally, IONA is still a work in progress. Although the core methodology exists, USIP welcomes feedback necessary to refine the process and its supporting tools, template, and database.

Rationale for the IONA Methodology

The end of the Cold War accelerated the use of media in peacebuilding. Without the discipline imposed by the two rival superpowers, competing ethnicities emerged as a cause of major conflicts in the post-Cold War world. First in Rwanda in 1994 and then in the Bosnia in 1995, ethnic cleansing and genocide became the defining characteristics of savage regional conflicts. In both cases, media played a disturbing role in accelerating the bloodshed. In response, the international community seized upon media as a policy tool with potentially great power to mend the causes of conflict.

Consequently, the past fifteen years have been a period of intensive experimentation in the application of media to peacebuilding. In Bosnia, the United Nations mandated regulatory changes curtailing hate speech; in Macedonia, the United States Agency for International Development (USAID) funded children's programming teaching conflict-resolution techniques; in Burundi, foreign nongovernmental organizations established a news organization staffed by both Hutu and Tutsi reporters and intended to deliver unbiased and independent news. Substantial funding has been injected into various conflict zones to support media interventions. However, these interventions have not always been effective.[1]

Evaluations of projects in the Balkans and elsewhere reveal various reasons why media interventions intended to promote Western democratic principles and media systems free from government control have not always achieved their objectives:

➤ Media alone cannot create social or political change.[2]

➤ Media intervention strategies have been designed quickly and under far-from-optimal conditions, such as during violent conflict.[3]

➤ Media practices are subordinate to political will rather than independent of political influence.[4]

Although all these observations are true, they are inadequate as operational explanations. If media alone cannot create social change, what else should intervention designers use to complement media-based activities? If media interventions must be designed quickly, how can we accelerate effective intervention planning? And if media activities occur in a politicized environment in combat zones, how should those politics inform the design of media interventions? The problem is not limitations of the media or the uncertainties of a conflict environment, but rather that interventions are developed using methods that cannot fully accommodate these constraints. What media scholar Robert Manoff observed at a USIP conference in 1997 is just as true today: media interventions for peacebuilding are characterized by the absence of a deliberate and systematic assessment methodology to determine the precise purpose of the specific intervention, why the intervention is needed, and exactly what the intervention must achieve.[5]

IONA seeks to address this problem by enabling a systematic definition of the target society's needs, the intervention's goals, and the criteria for successfully reaching those goals. IONA helps media experts define a media strategy that will effectively reduce conflict in a given society, or address a specific aspect of conflict such as corruption, displaced persons, or any number of issues. Using IONA, assessment teams should return from the field with an understanding of how targeted media investments will affect critical political and social problems. Additionally, with information acquired using IONA, funders can develop requests for proposal (RFPs) that clearly state what needs to be done, what success looks like, and how success will be measured during the implementation stage. By investing in an IONA-based planning study, donors can direct scarce resources to well-defined activities that evidence suggests will generate high returns. Furthermore, IONA findings help donors avoid those conflicts of interest in which implementers develop activities that better align with their own institutional capabilities than with the target society's needs. By defining how media consultants partner with donor organizations and how they identify potential media interventions, IONA seeks to ensure that both the donor organization and the target society get the media interventions that they need.

The community of consultants and experts that serve media donors also benefit from IONA. For those performing assessments, IONA offers a standardized approach that supports a rapid and efficient design of media interventions, a desirable outcome for what are typically fixed price consulting engagements. Implementing organizations may find that they can better respond to donor needs when RFPs reflect IONA's clearly defined outcomes. Finally, should media interventions become more effective as a result of IONA, it is reasonable to imagine that donors will look to media interventions more frequently as a means for reducing conflict.

Benefits of the IONA Methodology

IONA offers a systematic process for integrating conflict and media assessments. Table 1 compares the problems embodied in current methods for media assessment with the advantages obtained using the IONA solution.

Table 1. Media Assessment Problems and IONA Solutions

Media Assessment Problem	IONA Solution
The media are treated as a discrete, limited set of practices. Insufficient attention is paid to the social, economic, or political environment in which media exist and operate. Consequently, non-media factors undermine an intervention's effectiveness.	**IONA seeks to understand the media in a broad social, economic, and political context.** By considering media and non-media factors in the design of media interventions, IONA formally integrates a needs/conflict assessment (supporting the design of interventions that have a clear purpose) with a media assessment (supporting the design of interventions that are realistic and possible).
Outcomes are imprecisely defined. A methodology that produces poorly defined or overly ambitious objectives tends to result in interventions that are reactive or opportunistic rather than proactive and strategic.	**IONA precisely identifies the outcomes and the means to attain them.** Outcomes are defined as specific changes in knowledge, attitudes, and behaviors of target groups and are enabled by a well-defined set of activities.
Evaluation targets activities and processes, not outcomes. Because short-term activities and processes are easily measured, they are frequently confounded with the objectives of the intervention that these activities are meant to achieve.	**IONA explicitly ties media intervention outcomes to specific activities.** This approach enables intervention managers to measure and track aspects that are relevant to intervention outcomes.
Absence of a common methodology hinders effective coordination among implementing organizations. Lacking a common understanding among organizations in the field regarding an intervention's goals, implementers duplicate effort and even work at cross-purposes.	**IONA enables effective coordination among implementing organizations.** This methodology for the collection, organization, and analysis of data improves the quality and timeliness of results. Standardized data structures facilitate comparison across and between intervention studies.

IONA is **systematic and rigorous.** Because the methodology enforces information consistency, data collected during field interviews are entered into the framework and are immediately available for analysis.

This improves both the quality and the timeliness of the analysis and its results. Further, as an **integrated** tool that combines a needs assessment with a media assessment, IONA generates interventions that are both purposeful and possible. It is **outcomes oriented.** By recommending interventions that have been assessed as both purposeful and possible, IONA helps increase the effect of donor investment. Finally, IONA is **formative**. It helps donors make sound decisions about media interventions before human or financial resources have been committed to implementing an activity.

IONA is intended to be accessible and useful to organizations that implement media interventions in conflict-affected environments. With repeated use, media intervention practitioners and donors will create a large database of case studies that can be analyzed to discern qualities of successful and unsuccessful media interventions in fragile societies. IONA tools, instructions, and other resources can be accessed at http://www.usip.org/publications/iona.

Overview of the IONA Methodology

To improve the effectiveness of media interventions, the IONA process builds interventions that are both purposeful (that is, they address issues of high importance) and possible (they have a high likelihood of success). For media interventions to reach their objectives consistently, they must be predicated on the answers to a set of three questions:

1. What are the capabilities of the media sector in the society under study?

2. What do people in a fragile environment identify as the most significant causes of a given problem?

3. For each problem, which solutions are practicable, and which kinds of media interventions are most likely to facilitate achieving that solution?

These three questions can be further elaborated to the following:

1.a What media exist?

1.b How do those media affect their audiences?

2.a What social problems cause instability or conflict and require change?

2.b Which groups in society are most affected by these problems?

3.a What activities will most likely realize the desired changes?

3.b Who will make the desired change take place?

3.c How can the media be used to facilitate the desired change?

3.d How can the media be changed to enable the desired change?

IONA provides a systematic approach to collecting and analyzing the information necessary to answer these eight questions and create a portfolio of important and effective media interventions.

Questions 1.a and 1.b define a baseline of the media capabilities in the society. What are the primary media channels? What segments of society do these channels reach? What kind of content is broadcast within those channels? How does that content affect different segments within the audience? Because IONA is designed to develop media interventions to support social change, the assessment team must begin with an understanding of what impact the media is currently having in the society under study.

Questions 2.a and 2.b allow the assessment team to identify the purposeful or important problems to target. That is, what media interventions can be designed for this society that target the problems identified? In most cases, these questions will surface issues for which media's capabilities should be used as a tool and applied to create social change. In the case of media, though, these questions will identify issues that prevent it from being an effective tool for social change and thus make it a target for social change.

Finally, questions 3.a, 3.b, 3.c, and 3.d enable the assessment team to develop a media strategy and a set of activities that offer the best chance of overcoming specific problems facing society and bringing about the desired changed.

To answer these questions, IONA uses the three-stage process shown in figure 1. In the first stage, Defining the Assessment, the assessment team works with the donor organization to scope the assessment, develop a best guess as to the nature of the media landscape and conflict environment, and create an interview strategy to test these hypotheses. As a general rule, IONA requires assessment teams to do much work early in the assessment process, leaving the later stages for validation and testing. In the second

Figure 1. IONA Staging

Stage 1: Defining the Assessment
Perform initial conflict and media analyses to focus on fieldwork.

Step 1: Define the Scope of Work	Work with study sponsor to define issues to include in the assessment scope
Step 2: Profile the Media Landscape	Develop a comprehensive profile of the current media landscape in the fragile society
Step 3: Identify Issues	Identify issues that foster conflict and make a "best guess" as to the problems, needs, and objectives associated with each
Step 4: Create an Interview Strategy	Develop an interview strategy to investigate and evaluate each issue

Stage 2: Interviewing Respondents
Interview to validate and expand initial conflict and media analyses.

Step 1: Validate Media Profile	Interview media experts to verify accuracy of the media landscape profile
Step 2: Validate and Rank Issues	Interview media experts to identify the high importance issues that generate the most conflict
Step 3: Contextualize Issues of High Importance	Interview stakeholders to understand in-depth the problems, needs, obstacles, and activities that define issues of high importance
Step 4: Convert Reported Needs into Intervention Objectives	Reconcile conflicting needs reported in interviews to create objectives for media interventions that build peace
Step 5: Enroll In-Country Experts as Advisers	Identify in-country experts to evaluate final media intervention designs

Stage 3: Designing Media Interventions
Use interview data to create effective, integrated media interventions.

Step 1: Finalize Intervention Objectives	Continue synthesis of needs to identify objectives that build peace
Step 2: Design Media Interventions	Select media activities that realize intervention objectives

| | Step 3: Validate Interventions with Experts | Receive feedback from in-country experts evaluating effectiveness of intervention designs |
| | Step 4: Report Results | Write up assessment for publication |

stage, Interviewing Respondents, the assessment team enters the field to confirm what it has learned about the media and to determine the important issues confronting the target society and the corresponding objectives that will address these needs. By the end of the second stage, the assessment team has developed an understanding of media capabilities and potential intervention objectives. In the final stage, Designing Media Interventions, the assessment team develops media interventions by specifying those activities that will most likely realize the assessment's objectives.

In terms of how it collects and frames data, IONA does not distinguish between media and other institutions that play a positive or negative role in society; that is, the media undergo the same kind of examination and analysis as other social institutions. In assessing which tools to use to address conflict-related issues, however, it is important to recognize that media can simultaneously create problems and be part of the solution to other problems. In addition, media are only one of various tools that may be required for solving a conflict issue.

Likewise, IONA does not presume that media-based solutions are superior to others or that the media can or should replace other approaches to addressing a problem. We believe that IONA enables the assessment team to design media-based solutions with the greatest chance of achieving their objectives. At that same time, because IONA builds interventions based on issues identified in a conflict/needs assessment, the assessment team understands where and how their intervention can—and should—be effectively integrated with other kinds of interventions.

The IONA Framework

At the core of the IONA methodology is a data framework designed to capture social change. During a media assessment, the assessment team uses the IONA framework to organize information about social transformations that have already occurred in the target society. More importantly, the framework helps the team identify transitions that need to occur in order to achieve certain objectives that may help to reduce conflict and build peace.

The framework comprises six sets of components that define the desired social transformation. Shown in figure 2, these components are (1) the transformation from problem to objective (or need) defined in terms of knowledge, attitudes, and behaviors (KAB), (2) obstacles that block that transformation, (3) facilitators that enable it, (4) the position on the Change Ladder, (5) the level of analysis, and finally (6) solutions activities, that is, activities designed to enable these changes and eliminate obstacles.

Knowledge, Attitudes, and Behaviors

In describing the transformation of an issue from a problem state (one that causes conflict) to an objective state (one that builds peace), both the problem and objective states are defined in terms of the KAB of targeted groups in a society.[6] Knowledge, attitudes, and behaviors are defined as follows:

➤ **Knowledge** is what people in the target society know be true based on cognitive rather than emotional responses.

➤ **Attitudes** are what a people in the target society believe. These are often the reasons why certain knowledge is deemed important or why people engage in certain behaviors.

Figure 2. IONA Framework

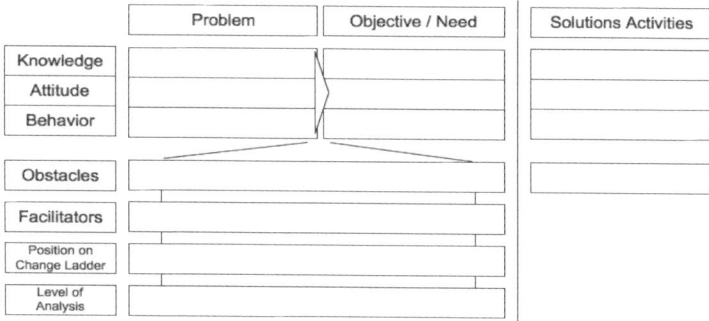

> **Behaviors** are what people in the target society do. Behavior is knowledge and attitudes made manifest in context, though not always with deliberate intent.

Although knowledge, attitudes, and behaviors can interconnect in various ways, IONA does not always assume a causal relationship among them. It cannot be assumed, for example, that knowledge alone leads to behavior change. A child soldier who learns about an amnesty program will not necessarily stop fighting. At the same time, if a child soldier stops fighting following exposure to an amnesty media campaign, it cannot be assumed that this soldier stopped because of the campaign. In order to design the media campaign most likely to yield the intended outcome, the field team must identify which change in knowledge, if any, has the greatest likelihood of motivating which kinds of change, if any, in attitudes or behaviors.

Because the IONA framework structures input data (transformations that have happened and transformations that respondents hope will happen) and output data (transformations that will actively build the peace), the desired state in a transformation is termed either a need or an objective. A desired transformation described by a respondent is a need. After considering multiple interviews that report similar or conflicting needs, the assessment team synthesizes these discovered needs into an objective that respects the various needs of the different respondents and their communities.

Obstacles to Change

Interventions with objectives at the personal level may be stymied by risks or obstacles experienced at the group level. Similarly, intended outcomes sought at the group level may be thwarted by obstacles occurring at the societal level. Defined broadly, obstacles are individuals, groups, or institutions that endorse political, economic, social, and cultural practices that limit the possibility of a change taking place. To design successful media interventions, obstacles to change must be identified and then convinced, marginalized, or overcome.

Facilitators of Change

Facilitators are people, institutions, values, experiences, tools, or events that enable the intervention to meet the objective. A successful intervention does not require the identification and use of all facilitators; however, understanding relevant facilitators will increase the likelihood of a successful outcome.

Identifying where change has been successful in the past or where tangible gains have been generated as a result of social action are two basic strategies for uncovering facilitators. Successful facilitators for change in the past may be powerful facilitators for change in the present. At the same time, they may not be. Because an effective media intervention may be based on a strategy unimagined by respondents, the assessment team must also test hypothetical intervention strategies to identify new facilitators.

Position on the Change Ladder

Social change does not occur abruptly. Put another way, it is unlikely that current behaviors, no matter how problematic they may be, will be discarded without careful thought and testing. Thus, societies, groups within societies, and individuals move through a process of consideration, evaluation, and testing. An assessment team will develop more effective media interventions if it understands where in this process a society or a group within the society sits with regard to an issue.

The IONA framework posits social change as an incremental, nonlinear, four-stage process that culminates in permanent change (see table 2).[7] Nonlinearity means that at any stage of change, a person or community may decide that it is not possible or desirable to proceed and

Table 2. Four-Step Change Ladder

	Step 1	Step 2	Step 3	Step 4
Current state of stakeholders in society	Existing in the status quo	Knowing what's wrong with the status quo	Knowing an alternative to the status quo	Having changed the status quo
Action to reach next step	Questioning the status quo	Considering alternatives to the status quo	Trying alternatives to the status quo	

may return to a previous stage until a more opportune moment arises to try moving forward again.[8]

Field interviews enable the assessment team to understand a target group's current position on the Change Ladder regarding a given issue, as well as what interventions could be realistically implemented to help move the target group to the next step in the process. Combined with an understanding of what may prevent movement (obstacles) or what may accelerate movement (facilitators) along the Change Ladder, the team uses this information to develop interventions better suited to a society's current capacity for change.

The Change Ladder and the concepts embedded in it are a critical part of the interviewing process. Because the assessment team is investigating sensitive issues that drive conflict, the team should take care not to alienate respondents by beginning an interview suggesting that little has been done to address the problem. The IONA interview process starts by assuming that the society is in Step 4 of the Change Ladder and works backward toward Step 1. By assuming the best, the assessment team shows the respect that encourages an engaged respondent.

Levels of Analysis and Intervention Design

In most cases, the various problems that comprise an issue exist simultaneously at different societal levels. Problems must be defined and addressed at all relevant levels in a coherent and coordinated manner for an intervention to achieve its intended outcomes.

A well-designed and well-executed assessment will identify the levels of society that need to be targeted and the precise objectives for each level addressed by the intervention. The IONA methodology posits three ways in which KAB occur in a society.

➤ **Individual level.** This refers to changes in KAB that affect how people in the target society conceive of themselves as individuals. For example, an intervention may illustrate the deleterious effects of ethnic stereotyping, with the objective of changing each individual's attitudes and behaviors in relationship to individuals from other ethnic groups.

➤ **Interpersonal/group level.** Interventions at this level affect shared, assumed, or expected KAB that people or groups in the target society have for formal or informal groups. A strategy often used in interventions on this level changes group KAB by targeting the group's leadership or other key members. For instance, as a way of de-escalating conflict, one member of an editorial team may convince his/her colleagues to stop using language offensive to certain communities.

➤ **Societal/structural level.** This is the most difficult level at which to effect change because it targets how people conceive of themselves as a society. Generally, these are institutional interventions that affect society as a whole, such as passing and enforcing laws that ban hate speech in the media.

IONA requires the assessment team to understand how problematic KAB manifest at various levels of society. Are KAB held by an individual? For example, "I am a Pashtun, not an Afghan, so why should I vote in the coming parliamentary elections?" Are they shared by a certain group? "We farmers believe that NATO security operations are a threat to our traditional way of life." Or are the KAB engrained institutionally in society? "The law does not permit people of mixed race to vote." Because problems may manifest at multiple levels in a society, media interventions must comprise activities that address those levels.

Solutions Activities

Here the assessment team describes the actual activities that enable transformation in KAB: developing radio dramas with particular themes and target audiences, building radio infrastructure to broaden the reach of media to illiterate audiences, or broadcasting a roundtable discussion among religious leaders showing that in Islam a wide range of opinions exist on the issue of educating girls.

There are two types of solutions activities: issue activities and obstacle activities. Issue activities directly address the KAB that define the problem and enable the transformation to the objective KAB. Obstacle activities transform KAB that block social change. To extend an example from above, if the issue activity is building radio infrastructure in rural areas, an obstacle is sabotage of the facility by partisans. Obstacle activities could be (in addition to enhanced security features at the broadcast sites) facilitating discussion with community leaders and designing pertinent programming to ensure strong community support for the radio towers.

The IONA Process

As a deliverable to the donor funding the intervention, IONA produces ten or perhaps a dozen potential interventions organized around the IONA framework. Many more potential interventions (and frameworks) are discarded as insufficiently important in reducing conflict or insufficiently possible in the current environment. Even more transformations are captured in the framework during field interviews as the basis for a fuller understanding of the conflict issues.

The IONA process is intended to manage the collection and synthesis of information describing the media, the conflict, and the relationship between the two. Because conflicts are complex and resources to understand them are limited, the process continually demands that the assessment team target only those issues, problems, objectives, and solutions (depending on the stage) that could reasonably produce a purposeful and possible intervention.

The IONA process comprises the following three stages:

1. Defining the Assessment
2. Interviewing Respondents
3. Designing Media Interventions

These stages are elaborated below.

Stage 1: Defining the Assessment

In the first stage of IONA, and before entering the field, the assessment team works closely with the project manager for the funding organization to do the following

1. Define the scope of work for the assessment;

2. Develop a comprehensive profile of the media landscape and capabilities;

3. Identify issues; and

4. Create an interviewing strategy to understand issues in greater detail.

These steps are explained below.

Define the Scope of Work

The scope of work (SOW) defines which issues will be included in the assessment and which will not. It is developed in collaboration with the assessment sponsor and is based on sponsor goals. The IONA methodology is intended to yield interventions that address needs articulated by the broadest range of stakeholders associated with the target issues at hand. Nevertheless, sponsors may want to focus the scope of an IONA assessment based on several considerations, such as the following:

➤ Targeted issues (for example, issues directly related to physical security)

➤ Events (such as interventions to encourage participation in an election)

➤ Geography (interventions to address instability in rural regions)

➤ Media type (interventions that are performed using cell phones)

➤ Media audience (interventions that affect women and their roles in a society)

➤ Budget constraints for intervention (intervention activities designed in the assessment can cost no more than $X million)

➤ Time constraints for intervention (intervention activities designed in the assessment must be complete by a certain date)

➤ Pre-existing program portfolio (interventions must complement a broader country strategy that is already in place)

➤ Pre-existing donor partnerships (only issues that build on pre-existing government, NGO, or diplomatic relationships)

IONA was designed to work within various parameters. Depending on sponsor needs, for example, the methodology can by applied to an entire society in conflict, or it can focus on specific issues in specific locales, such as how to use media to ameliorate tension caused by the arrival of internally displaced people in an urban area. The sponsoring organization may already have a plan that outlines its assessment of the issues facing the target society, and how the donor would like to go about addressing these issues.

Regardless, the assessment team must understand the SOW and the ramifications of any limits set on the issues, problems, and objectives defining potential interventions. In general, as the SOW narrows, more specific problems, objectives, and solutions can be generated in the assessment. For example, at the regional level, the assessment team could obtain nuanced views about girls' education from specific community leaders or particular media owners. With more granular information, the resulting media intervention becomes more specific in terms of potential partners, messages, and target audiences.

The SOW should allow a reasonable amount of time and devote sufficient personnel to the task. These issues are discussed in the Requirements section below.

Profile the Media Landscape

Next, the team will review the literature and interview subject matter experts in order to develop a profile of the target society's media. The object is to identify, to the extent possible, existing strengths and weaknesses of the media sector in the target country. Such a profile includes which media exist, who uses them, whom particular media serve, media content, media ownership, financing, level of professionalization, and media regulation. Potential resources in creating this profile include online reports by other organizations, papers published in academic journals, experts from the media industry or academia, government white papers, and trade association publications.

Some data may not be accessible to the research team while it is not in the field. This could include common media consumption habits of the target population, specific programs aired, and the programming media consumers would like to have but which is not presently available. Furthermore, various contradictions may emerge during desk research that will have to be clarified in the field. In the early stage of the fieldwork (Stage 2), the assessment team will collect this information and validate what it already knows. Appendix A provides a framework for collecting this data.

When completed, the profile should give the assessment team a general sense of the capabilities of the target society's media with respect to the conflict; that is, where media could be used as a constructive element in social transformation, and where media contribute to social fragility and conflict. If time and resources permit, the assessment team may elect to outsource the development of this profile to an in-country organization specializing in media.

Where the media can be used as a tool for social change, it is sufficient for the team to leave its assessment of the media at the level of description. If the team determines that some portion of the media are creating conflict or blocking positive social change, the team needs to flag this in order to develop an issue tree as preparation to possibly populating an IONA frame targeting transformation of some aspect of the media (see below for information on creating issue trees).

The media profile is a deliverable to the sponsor organization. It is an interim deliverable; that is, it is information that must be reported to the sponsor's project manager to show that the study is on course. It is not, however, the answer to the study. The media profile should summarize and communicate what has been learned but need not be of publication quality. It is a working document.

Identify Issues

The goal of this step is to list issues inside and outside the media sector that create fragility in the portion of the society defined by the SOW. The team makes best guesses about the issues, sub-issues, problems, and needs causing fragility in the target society. This step will result in preliminary issue trees (see figure 3). An issue tree comprises (1) issues, (2) sub-issues, (3) problems, and (4) objectives.

Developing issue trees during Stage 1 organizes initial research about issues and sub-issues that can be preliminarily linked to problems and objectives in IONA frames.

➤ **Issues.** Implicit in the SOW document will be a set of issues relevant to the interests of the sponsor. Using online reports, academic papers,

Figure 3. IONA Issue Tree

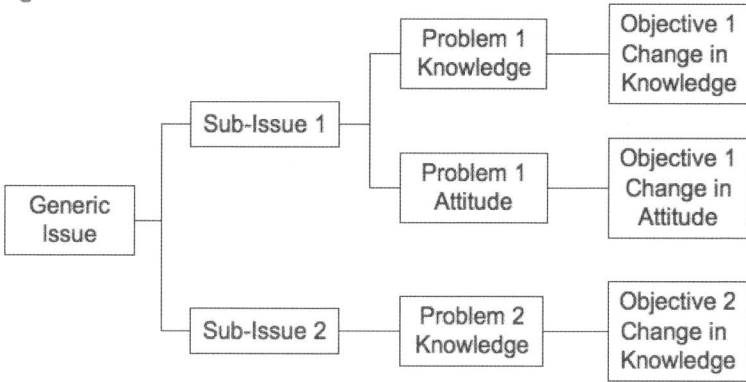

interaction with experts on the conflict, and government white papers, the assessment team identifies related issues and relevant sub-issues. The assessment team will estimate which issues and sub-issues are of high importance.

➤ **Problems.** The assessment team should attempt to describe the high-importance issues and sub-issues in terms of the KAB held by actors in the target society. This will be the team's best guess as to how individuals currently experience the issue (or sub-issue) in their daily lives. Even using all research resources available, the assessment team may not be able to define the associated problem completely.

➤ **Objectives.** Where possible, the assessment team should develop hypotheses regarding the frame objective to be associated with each problem. Like the problems developed above, the objectives are defined in terms of KAB. The research team may be able to guess at other framework elements that comprise a hypothetical transformation around an important issue or sub-issue.

As a general rule, at this stage of the assessment the list of issues and sub-issues will be the most developed and longest, and the corresponding list of objectives will be the least defined and shortest.

The process of focusing the assessment team's research efforts is crucial to successfully designing effective interventions. Focusing too soon risks missing something important; focusing too late risks investing too much effort on dead-end issues and sub-issues. Even after pruning according to sponsor interests, the list of issues facing a fragile society can be long. The assessment team should identify which issues or related sub-issues are of high importance—that is, which issues the team believes warrant additional investigation—and why. Although the prioritization of issues will be subjective, the following criteria can be applied to assess their relative importance:

➤ The **frequency** an issue is mentioned in the literature. Generally, an issue that is mentioned frequently is going to be highly important.

➤ The **credibility** of the source mentioning a particular issue. If an issue is mentioned only once but by a highly credible respondent, the issue may warrant inclusion.

➤ The **altitude** of the issue; that is, whether it is localized or pertains more broadly. Assessing altitude is critical because an issue identified in literature about a specific zone or region (for example, poppy cultivation in southern Afghanistan) may not pertain to other parts of the country. Likewise, an issue that is identified as affecting all segments of the population (for example, corruption in Afghanistan) will manifest differently in specific local contexts.

➤ The **recency** of the source mentioning an issue. Because conflict dynamics are fluid, something that was indisputably accurate only a few years ago may no longer be true, or as true, now.

At the conclusion of this work, generally about one quarter (or at least ten) of the issues or sub-issues identified should be marked as high importance. The assessment team will have begun converting what it has learned from the literature and from discussions with subject matter experts into the IONA frame of problems and objectives based on KAB, obstacles, and facilitators. *The goal is not to find the answer to the assessment before entering the field but rather to organize the knowledge obtained so far and to develop hypotheses about the problems and objectives corresponding to the issues the assessment is targeting.* Neither the sponsor nor the assessment team should get too attached to any specific issue, problem, or objective at this stage as the fieldwork may refute the validity of the team's preliminary conclusions.

Create an Interview Strategy

Because interviews are the primary means by which an assessment team develops and validates media assessments, careful preparation during Stage 1 is vital to a successful assessment. This preparation has three interrelated elements: (1) the interview strategy, (2) the interview guides, and (3) the interview roster.

Interview Strategy

The interview strategy is a written description of how the team will collect the information necessary to complete the assessment. It defines what groups will need to be interviewed within the target society and explains why their input is important. Having defined the important groups to interview, sufficient interviews must be planned and undertaken in each interview group.

There are three types of interviews undertaken during the interviewing process: (1) interviews with media experts to validate the media profile; (2) interviews with individuals having sufficient perspective on the problems facing the target society to validate the relative importance of the identified issues and sub-issues; and (3) interviews with representatives of different groups in society to develop a deeper understanding of specific high-importance issues and their associated problems, needs, obstacles and facilitators of change, and potential solutions.

The interview strategy should also provide a rough idea of how many interviews will be performed and how many of that total will be assigned to each interview type (along with a rationale explaining the allocation). What constitutes a sufficient number will vary, but five interviews per group is reasonable. This provides a sufficient sample to understand and check the position of the majority of the group and to identify the presence of any large minority positions. Interviewers can reasonably conduct about two interviews per day, including preparation and post-interview work.

The interview strategy should also outline what special resources will be required to conduct these interviews. Will the interview team require special transportation? Are introductions necessary (and, if so, from whom)? Will translators be required? Is an exchange of gifts an important preliminary to meaningful discussion (and, if so, what sort of gifts)? If the society is in conflict, are security precautions necessary (and, if so, how will this affect the interviews)? Perhaps most importantly, who is best suited to conduct the interviews to ensure their authenticity? Populations living in conflict environments are notoriously difficult to poll or to interview with confidence.

Interview Guides

Because each interview type has a different goal, it requires a different type of interview guide. Appendix B contains a generic interview guide to identify and validate high-importance issues, and appendix C contains a generic interview guide that contains questions that map to the IONA frame.

The questions in these interview guides are intended to help the assessment team decide what types of questions to ask various respondents. They should not to be used literally in the field. Before bringing actual interview questions into the field, the team should consult with a social scientist who is from the target society or who is an expert in that society to ensure that the interview questions will make sense to potential respondents. The expert may be able to offer advice on word selection as well as on the general interviewing approach.

As part of developing an effective interview strategy, the assessment team must understand how to approach sensitive issues. The role of Islam in girls' education is an obvious example of how an interviewer could quickly alienate a respondent. For example, an interviewer in Afghanistan may suspect that radical clerics have a major role in blocking girls' access to education. The interviewer, however, cannot simply ask, "Why does Islam not permit girls to go to school?" Rather, the topic must be approached indirectly: "What does Islam say about education?" "What kind of education does Islam say girls should receive?" "How does girls' schooling differ between the Taliban period and the present?" Islam is not identified as the problem, but as a factor in education that needs to be understood. Collaborating with an expert on the target society will facilitate converting the generic interview guides provided in appendices B and C into effective guides grounded in the social, cultural, and political expectations of the target society.

When using the interview guides, the team must decide how much of the analytic framework to reveal. In interviews with social scientists or with individuals who understand some or all of the team's approach, a description of IONA methodology and the associated four-step change process can help accelerate data collection. In interviews with individuals having less or no familiarity with social science methods, the interviewer must decide how to use the IONA frame as a guide. It is important to underline here that IONA is very much grounded in the "design backward, implement forward" approach. Hence, the questions in the guidelines are also structured in a way that works backward from eliciting the future state desired by respondents, to asking how respondents think it possible to arrive at that future state, and asking for examples of previous attempts to create change (successful or not). This approach to interviewing may not always succeed because the ways people think about themselves in time and place vary extensively. It may be necessary to structure the questions entirely sequentially, starting with understanding the present and working forward incrementally until there is a thorough comprehension of the desired future state. In developing the IONA interview guides, it is crucial to make the questions meaningful to the respondents.

Interview Roster

The list of potential respondents should include individuals who can address the issues identified in the SOW. Media experts and conflict experts may be especially important respondents early in fieldwork to confirm the media profile and the preliminary issue hypotheses. Proposed interviews should be classified into one of the three different interview types described above. As a rule, at least 75 percent of the interviews should be allotted to the third type that develop a deeper understanding of specific high-importance issues and their associated problems, needs, obstacles and facilitators of change, and potential solutions.

Stage 2: Interviewing Respondents

Fieldwork is the crux of applying IONA. The five steps in this stage are as follows:

1. Validate media profile

2. Validate and rank the issues

3. Contextualize issues of high importance

4. Convert reported needs into intervention objectives

5. Enroll in-county experts as advisors

These steps are explained below.

Validate Media Profile

The assessment team arrives in the field with a detailed but preliminary profile of the media landscape generated through desk research. These findings are refined through meetings with key respondents who have knowledge of the media sector in the target society. Potential respondents could include those working in the media itself (particularly owners, editors, operators), donor and nongovernmental organizations with histories of working with the media in the target society (such as press officers as well as staff responsible for media-related program work), and media consumers who can articulate a user perspective on media patterns. Any changes to the desk-based media profile that emerges from these interviews should be incorporated into the media profile document as soon as is practically possible.

Because media is both a tool to transform society and also an institution that may need to be targeted for transformation, the assessment team attending these interviews should be prepared to perform both types of interviews. All interviews with media experts should begin as an opportunity to test the validity of the media profile developed in Stage 1. However, the discussion may move toward issues faced by the media industry, in which case the interview team should be prepared to perform an interview designed to identify the sub-issues and associated problems, needs, obstacles, facilitators, and potential solutions.

At the completion of each interview, the interviewer updates a spreadsheet designed to track interviews and compares it to the goals established in the interview strategy. Each interview should record the respondent's name, title, affiliation, contact information, interview date, interview type (media validation, issue validation, issue contextualization), interview group, and the file name for interview notes.

Validate and Rank Issues

The assessment team enters the field with a comprehensive list of the issues facing the target society and a general idea about which issues would rank in the top quartile (or, at minimum, the top 10 issues) in terms of importance. In order to focus the assessment quickly, within the first week of fieldwork the assessment team must validate and rank the list of high-importance issues by interviewing individuals with sufficient breadth of experience in the issues identified. Potential respondents include senior government ministers, university professors, and senior nonprofit executives, to name just a few examples.

Because such individuals may have in-depth information regarding a particular high-importance issue, the assessment team should attend these interviews prepared to build out an issue tree and perform an interview designed to identify the sub-issues and associated problems, needs, obstacles, facilitators, and potential solutions. Each IONA frame developed with respect to an issue or sub-issue inherits the estimated importance of the issue or sub-issue. Because IONA currently uses a spreadsheet to manage frame data (and in the future will use custom software to do the same), a numeric rating of the importance of an issue or sub-issue is used to identify and order important issues and sub-issues, and, eventually, the interventions. Following each interview, the assessment team will rate the importance of the issue to the target society as well as the credibility of the respondent on that issue. Both scores are estimates by the assessment team using the scorecards shown in table 3. Because the credibility scoring depends on how representative the respondent's insights are of his or her group, as the interview team develops a better sense of each group's views, the team may have to revisit earlier interviews and rescore them for credibility.

Again, the assessment team should update the interview spreadsheet with the relevant information.

Contextualize Issues of High Importance

Once the set of high-importance issues are validated and well defined, the assessment team conducts another type of interview to develop a full understanding of the problems, needs, obstacles, facilitators, and solutions corresponding to an issue or sub-issue. In short, for each interview the team will collect information that will be entered into one or more IONA frameworks depending on the number of examples of social transformation (already undertaken or desired in the future) communicated during an interview.

Respondents in this stage should have deep, issue-specific expertise. Potential respondents include international and domestic media professionals, university professors, or leaders from civil society, government (local, national, and supranational), and communities.

Table 3. Scoring for IONA Issue Importance and Respondent Credibility

Importance
1   Resolution of this issue will have no impact on the fragility of the targeted portion of society.
2   Resolution of this and other equally important issues will marginally reduce the fragility in the targeted portion of society.
3   Resolution of this and other equally important issues will substantially reduce the fragility in the targeted portion of society.
4   Resolution of this issue and several subsidiary issues will substantially reduce the fragility in the targeted portion of society.
5   Resolution of this issue alone will substantially reduce the fragility in the targeted portion of society.

Credibility
1   This person represents only his or her own perceptions accurately.
2   This person sometimes accurately represents the perceptions of his or her group.
3   This person accurately represents the perceptions of his or her group.
4   This person sometimes accurately represents the perceptions of his or her society.
5   This person accurately describes his or her society without bias.

In this stage, the assessment team is trying to understand how far along the change process the society has progressed regarding a particular issues or sub-issue. In most cases, the society will have had some success in making changes to KAB that are necessary to reach its goals. At the same time, in its current state, the target society may have failed at least once to make KAB changes necessary to progress further. For example, if on a particular issue, a target society has progressed to Step 2 on the Change Ladder, the respondent will report that the society has had some success in making the changes in KAB required to question the status quo. At the same time, the respondent may report multiple failures in developing the KAB necessary to understand what alternative it faces to the status quo, which is Step 3 on the Change Ladder. Any designed media intervention must target the position on the Change Ladder where the target society has failed to advance.

For each success or failure in social transformation described by the respondent, the team is expected to understand the change in the KAB identified; the obstacles that prevented realization of that change; the facilitators that enabled the change; the level in the society where the change was expected, and the solutions activities that were attempted. Of particular interest to the assessment team will be the needs articulated for failed transformations. These needs, in conjunction with similar needs reported in other interviews, will become the basis for an intervention developed to address the associated issue or sub-issue.

For each social transformation attempted, the respondent will describe the activities undertaken by society. The assessment team must categorize the activities as either issue activities or obstacle activities. Each type of intervention activity has a target. In the case of issue activities, the targets are the KAB that create conflict; in the case of obstacle activities, the targets are the KAB that block the desired social transformation. Any attempted transformation, whether a success or failure, must be formally captured in the IONA frame, tagged by issue, by interview, and by interviewers.

Because IONA evaluates potential media interventions in terms both of importance and effectiveness, each frame is tagged with information concerning the transformation's importance. Each solutions activity described in the frame is assigned an estimated effectiveness score. How well did it dispose of its target? If the activity's target was to show parents how other parents risk educating their daughters, how effective was a Public Service Announcement (PSA) campaign in changing the parents' attitudes on the risks they face in sending their daughters to school? The assessment team estimates both the effectiveness of the activity and the credibility of the respondent. Both scores are estimates by the assessment team using the scorecards shown in table 4.

Finally, after each interview (preferably, no later than the evening of the interview), the interviewers must transfer the insights from the interview into their IONA database and update the interview spreadsheet.

Convert Reported Needs into Intervention Objectives

IONA creates media interventions based on the needs reported by respondents with respect to particular issues. Because those needs may be contradictory—the society, after all, is in conflict—the assessment team

Table 4. Scoring for IONA Solutions Activity Effectiveness and Respondent Credibility

	Effectiveness
1	This activity is not effective in disposing of its target.
2	This activity slightly disposes of its target.
3	This activity partially disposes of its target.
4	This activity mostly disposes of its target.
5	This activity completely disposes of its target.

	Credibility
1	This person learned about this solutions activity in discussion with a third party (such as at a conference or from a colleague).
2	This person learned about this solutions activity in publication from a third party (such as a newspaper).
3	This person learned about this solutions activity from a direct participant in the solutions activity.
4	This person learned about this solutions activity from an internal report on the solutions activity.
5	This person directly participated in the solutions activity.

must convert the needs reported during interviewing into objectives for potential media interventions.

To do this, the assessment team collects all failed frames relevant to a particular issue or sub-issue. The needs described in these frames may be very similar or they may be very different. Where there is agreement on what needs to be done, the objective is easily defined by the assessment team. More often, however, because different groups in society have different and conflicting interests, the assessment team must identify an intervention objective that can resolve the conflict implicit in those identified needs. In defining a desired social transformation for an issue, the assessment team should review information concerning obstacles and facilitators.

In reframing reported needs as intervention objectives, the assessment team will also have some insight into how to realize the objective.

Although a formal analysis that links solutions activities to social transformation is a Stage 3 activity, the assessment team is expected to have preliminary hypotheses ready at the end of Stage 2 as to what solutions activities (issue and obstacle) will realize the desired social transformations.

Enroll In-Country Experts as Advisers

As the interview process proceeds, some respondents will stand out in particular for the depth of their insight, their ability to adequately represent members of an interview group, or their knowledge of or connectedness to media in the target society. The assessment team should enroll these individuals as experts to consult in Stage 3. Because the assessment team will no longer be in the field when these experts are needed, these individuals must have the capacity to respond relatively quickly (by phone or e-mail) to queries from the assessment team. In some cases, a stipend may be required to guarantee action.

The experts on this list have the following two tasks with respect to the interventions developed in Stage 3:

➤ They must be able to provide insight into whether the new KAB proposed as intervention objectives are likely to be acceptable to various groups in the society.

➤ They must be able to provide insight into how well the solutions activities comprising the proposed intervention will enable the transformation of KAB (both issues and obstacles).

No individual will possess expertise across the entire scope of the study.

In summary, with respect to high-importance issues and sub-issues, the assessment team should leave the field knowing the following:

➤ KAB that define the problem

➤ KAB that define the change that will realize the objective

➤ Obstacles to that change

➤ Facilitators of that change

➤ Target society's position on the Change Ladder

➤ Target group for that change

➤ Activities that have brought the target society to this point in the four-stage change process, and why

➤ Activities that have failed to successfully realize the needed change, and why

➤ Preliminary guesses as to the solutions activities that will realize the intervention objective

Based on this information, the assessment team will be well positioned to develop high-impact media interventions.

Stage 3: Designing Media Interventions

The goal of the final stage of IONA is to develop effective media interventions. Tasks for this stage are the following:

1. Finalize intervention objectives

2. Design media interventions that meet objectives

3. Validate interventions with experts

4. Report results

These steps are explained below.

Finalize Intervention Objectives

The team continues the work begun in Stage 2 in synthesizing reported needs into intervention objectives. Because the assessment team will probably perform interviews until the last moment in the field, this activity must be extended into Stage 3. Furthermore, defining intervention objectives is difficult work that requires careful understanding and an ability to balance the different interests around an issue or sub-issue. The assessment team consequently will require some time to think.

Design Media Interventions That Meet Objectives

For each high-importance issue or sub-issue, the problem, objective, obstacles, and facilitators are now well defined. The assessment team develops a media intervention for each high-importance objective by defining solutions activities that will effectively realize the desired objective.

Four sources of insight can assist the assessment team in developing sets of solutions activities to realize these objectives:

➤ **Respondent insight.** For each issue, the problem, objective, obstacles, facilitator, and solutions provided by the respondents are the basis for designing a successful media intervention. Respondents have invaluable insight into what has worked and has not worked in their own society around any given issue or sub-issue.

➤ **Assessor insight.** Based on experience in the application of media to conflict, the assessment team will have insight into what media interventions have worked in addressing conflict in similar circumstances elsewhere in the world.

➤ **Published insight.** The assessment team can search the literature describing what other media interventions have been implemented and how they have transformed targeted societies.

➤ **IONA insight.** USIP will manage a database of IONA-based interventions. The assessment team will be able to search this database to learn about comparable issues in other societies, the recommended interventions, and their effectiveness. Identical data structures based on the IONA frame will enable a rapid comparison of the given issue to successful past IONA interventions.

For comparability, solutions activities based on assessor insight, published insight, and IONA insight will require the assessment team to consult the expert panel to determine how the non-native activity would be organized in the target society, and what its estimated effectiveness would be.

As the assessment team identifies potential media solutions activities, it must ensure that all proposed activities are based on capabilities defined in the updated profile of the media landscape. Information collected while validating the media profile should have identified media issues that will be obstacles to realizing particular objectives. To avoid oversights, however, the assessment team must cross-reference known media issues and problems against all proposed solutions to ensure that the media capabilities required are present despite societal conflict.

Figure 4. Purposeful and Possible Media Interventions

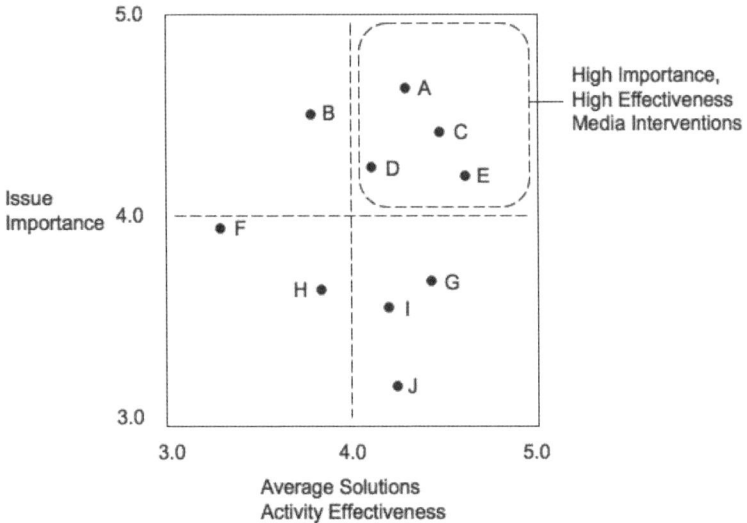

The assessment team may find that a desired social change may not be achievable using media activities alone. Especially around behavior change, the solution best suited to a successful intervention is likely to be an opportunity to apply knowledge (in a non-media experience) rather than the consumption of knowledge (in a media experience). Thus, solutions activities within a media intervention can be a mixture of media and non-media activities. For example, in an area where longstanding tensions between two competing ethnic groups have erupted into conflict over water rights, a shared water management project becomes not simply a material solution to the water shortages but also opportunity to build trust by applying knowledge communicated in a complementary media campaign.

Furthermore, not all objectives will have a solution that is practicable in the current state of the target society. At the present time, with the available resources, the desired social change may just not be possible. The assessment team must make its best deduction about which solutions are possible under current circumstances. Solutions deemed impossible are not worth pursuing.

In evaluating the media interventions developed using IONA, each intervention will address an issue or sub-issue with an estimated importance attached to it. Likewise, each intervention will include a set of solutions activities whose numeric scores can be averaged to produce an estimate of the likely success of the intervention. As an aid to identifying desirable interventions, a scatterplot helps identify graphically those interventions that are most important to the society and most likely to work. Figure 4 shows ten interventions (A-J) presented on a graph. The average solutions activity effectiveness for each intervention forms the x-axis, and issue importance forms the y-axis. Interventions that occupy the upper right quadrant of the plot have the highest combined scores in terms of importance in reducing conflict (purpose) and the likelihood of successful realization (possibility).

Educating Young Women: An Example from Afghanistan

Figure 5 shows a completed IONA frame for one issue related to the status of women in a targeted society. This example showing the linkage between issues, problems, objectives, and solutions in an IONA frame comes from an assessment performed by USIP in Afghanistan in 2009. The KAB that form the problem (girls not going to school) stem from parents' KAB about their female children. The intended outcome (objective or desired change) is that parents send their girls to school. The IONA frame identifies the primary obstacle to this change as radical clerics' religious objections to female education combined with parents' belief that their religious leaders must be obeyed because such leaders are the recognized arbiters of Islamic doctrine. This parental attitude overrides other considerations about whether girls should go to school. The frame also identifies a different group of religious leaders, teachers, and community leaders who advocate female education and therefore may serve as facilitators of the desired change. The solution consists of issue activities intended to change parents' knowledge and attitudes about what their daughters can and cannot do, and why; and obstacle activities designed to change parents' attitudes and behavior regarding the authority of certain religious leaders (for example, by illustrating options that parents may not have considered). Taken together, these media activities constitute a potential media intervention to enable young girls to receive an education.

Figure 5. Completed IONA Frame and Associated Intervention

ISSUE: Women are not equal to men in target society.

SUB-ISSUE: Girls do not receive an education because parents do not send them to school.

	Problem	Objective	Solution Activities
Knowledge	Parents know radical clerics will condemn them if they send their girls to school.	Parents know other families have risked radical clerics' anger by educating their girls.	*Issue Activities:* Air PSA radio campaign targeting parental knowledge (show what other families have risked to educate their girls) and attitudes toward female education (change belief that education threatens their daughters' ability to marry).
Attitudes	Parents believe educated girls can't marry well and the family will lose bride money.	Parents believe that their daughters' futures are more secure if they are educated.	
Behaviors	Parents flout the law that requires all children to be sent to school.	Parents abide by the law and send their daughters to school.	
Obstacles	Radical clerics reject girls' education as violating Islam. Parents believe such radical interpretations are the only legitimate ones.		*Obstacle Activity:* Air moderated radio discussions between pro- and con-religious leadership (change parents' view of clerical authority)
Facilitators	Clerics trained overseas who believe that girls should be educated, teachers who support girls' education, community leaders who want to undermine the authority of radical clerics.		
Position on Change Ladder	Step 3: Trying alternatives to the status quo		
Level of Analysis	Parents (individual, inter-group)		

Validate Interventions with Experts

While in the field, the assessment team selected particular individuals to act as expert advisors. The completed interventions are written up, ranked in terms of importance and effectiveness, and shared with these individuals.

At this late stage, the expert's role is not to opine on whether the team should have included other issues or sub-issues in the high-importance group that constituted the focus of the study. Instead, for each intervention, the expert is expected to:

➤ Evaluate the proposed social transformation. In their view, does the problem KAB constitute an important root cause of the issue? Is the transformation in KAB, proposed by the solution, the best solution available at present? Has the assessment team overlooked or underestimated the impact of an obstacle on this transformation?

➤ Evaluate the proposed activities designed to effect the social transformation. If implemented competently, are the proposed activities likely to bring about the desired change in KAB? Has the assessment team developed activities to eliminate or weaken obstacles to the proposed transformation? Do the necessary media capabilities to deliver these activities effectively exist in-country?

Because the experts are not above the politics that contribute to the conflict—especially if they were chosen on the basis of how well they represent a particular interview group—their responses should not be blindly accepted. However, if the assessment team chooses to ignore expert commentary, it must have a strong rationale detailing why the expert's insight has been rejected or modified.

Depending on the number of experts and the number of interventions, the assessment team may wish to target particular experts with particular interventions in order to avoid exhausting the expert's commitment to the assessment process. This process and its rationale should be shared with the assessment's sponsor.

Report Results

The analysis of intervention options is now complete. Each highly important issue or sub-issue is paired with the set of media activities most likely to realize the change in KAB that ameliorates that issue as a source of conflict in the target society.

Although each assessment team will want to develop its own report structure, a generic outline based on the various documents generated using IONA is presented in table 5. The Executive Summary and the Ten Best Media Interventions must be powerful and to the point. Busy executives in the sponsoring organization will want only the gist. The sections that follow the summary detail why the proposed interventions are important and effective. Sections 4a and 4b provide overviews of the entire target society, the issues that create conflict, and media capabilities. Sections 4c–4e focus the discussion on only the high-importance issues identified in 4a. (This parallels the focusing that occurs in Stages 2 and 3 of IONA).

Table 5. Generic Table of Contents for Assessment Report

Section	Title	Contents
1	Executive Summary	Brief review of the SOW and assessment results, including recommended interventions
2	Ten Best Media Interventions	Narrative descriptions of the ten most important and effective media strategies
3	Overview of the USIP IONA Methodology	Overview of IONA and its application to the issues identified in the SOW
4a	Issues Destabilizing the Target Society	Description of the high-importance issues identified by IONA
4b	Media Capabilities in the Target Society	Evaluation of the current media capabilities in the target society
4c	Reported Needs to Build Peace in the Target Society	Description of the needs reported during interviewing
4d	Social Transformation in the Target Society	Synthesis of reported needs into objectives, and description of obstacles to and facilitators for realizing these objectives
4e	Solutions Activities that Enable Social Transformation	Description and evaluation of the solutions activities that enable social transformation and remove obstacles
5	Conclusions	
Appendices	A: Updated Interview Strategy B: Updated Interview Guides C: Completed Interview List D: Expert List	

Conducting Analysis Using IONA

IONA is a method for collecting and organizing data. Its framework of issues, problems, objectives, and solutions activities are intended to capture the needs articulated by respondents around specific social problems. These needs are reduced to potential intervention objectives for which solutions activities are identified. Although this discipline ensures that all relevant data are at hand for analysis, it does not eliminate the need for creative and insightful analysis by the assessment team.

Beginning in Stage 2 and continuing in Stage 3, the assessment team is asked to create clarity out of the large body of information that is collected through the interview process. During Stage 2, the team receives numerous descriptions of needs, which must be reframed as objectives corresponding to concrete problems. During Stage 3, the team must take a large set of potential solutions and develop media intervention strategies that address the identified objectives.

IONA provides the data structure (or frame) that allows the assessment team to draw insight from the data quickly and effectively. By tagging individual pieces of data when they are entered into the frame, the assessment team can manipulate or cut the full body of collected information into different data clusters that can be compared and evaluated. For example, cutting the full body of information to include only data about one particular issue allows the assessment team to develop insight about the objectives for an intervention targeting that issue. Further cutting data by effectiveness will provide direction as to what activities have worked well in the past in addressing problems in this issue area. A common denominator may emerge that suggests a new solution to the problem that is currently confounding the target society. By iteratively cutting the entire data set, the assessment team can gain perspective on the issue and develop a successful media intervention strategy.

No matter how the assessment team organizes its data in practice (on notepads, in Word documents, in spreadsheets, and the like), at minimum the team needs to be able to tag and manipulate the information from its interviews with the following identifiers:

➤ Issue

➤ Problem

➤ Respondent

➤ Need

➤ Importance

➤ Effectiveness

Likewise, at minimum, to create the necessary data clusters for analysis, the assessment team must be able to manipulate data stored in IONA in the following ways:

➤ Filter

➤ Sort

➤ Search

➤ Compare

Developing this functionality using a paper-based approach is a major challenge. USIP has developed a spreadsheet-based prototype tool called IONA Frame Manager that overcomes many of the problems with a paper-based approach. Visit USIP's Center for Media, Conflict and Peacebuilding at http://www.usip.org/publications/iona to access to this tool.

Requirements for Analysis

The time and personnel required to perform an IONA study depend very much on the SOW. This is determined in negotiation with the organization sponsoring the assessment and is detailed in the SOW document developed during Stage 1 of the assessment process.

Time

Critical to the effectiveness of the assessment mission will be the allocation of sufficient time in Stage 1. Factors that influence the amount of time required include team member experience with the society under study, the amount of existing research, and access to others with experience in the target country. Similarly, the amount of time required in-country will be influenced by the ability to move around, access sectoral and thematic experts and communities themselves, and address any other logistic constraints. For example, the Afghanistan assessment was designed to take 3½ months, with five weeks allocated to each of the three stages. The Stage 3 analysis after returning from the field is not time consuming if care is taken to organize collected data during the fieldwork. Thus, the preliminary results of the assessment should be available within two to three weeks of returning from the field. However, validating intervention designs with in-country experts, getting sign-off on designs from the donor organization, and writing the assessment report can extend this stage substantially.

Personnel: Assessment Team

The assessment team as a whole should possess both conflict and media analysis skills. It is helpful if at least one member of the team has deep experience in the application of media to peacebuilding and another is experienced in conflict analysis. Specific understanding of the media in the target country is a benefit, but not absolutely required. Lack of knowledge, however, must be factored into the amount of time allowed for work prior to entering the field as well as for work in the field. Likewise, although contacts in-country are a plus, the presence on the team of someone with an extensive list of existing contacts cannot be expected. Making contact with in-country experts is part of the development of an interview strategy during Stage 1.

The assessment team should be independent of any organization currently implementing media interventions in the society to be assessed. This will ensure that the results are impartial and have greater credibility.

Personnel: Project Manager

The project manager is an employee of the organization sponsoring the assessment and is the single point of contact between the organization commissioning the assessment and the assessment team. As such, the project manager's responsibilities change during the assessment process.

During Stage 1, the primary tasks for the project manager are to communicate the sponsor's goals in defining the SOW, help the assessment team access various resources, and ensure the team is ready to work when they enter the field. For example, the project manager works closely with the assessment team to develop a well-defined SOW. The project manger also may have contacts in the field and can help develop an interview strategy.

In Stages 2 and 3, the primary task of the project manager is to ensure that the project team is making progress and reaching the milestones defined in the IONA process. The manager continues to provide insight and other resources as the assessment team's understanding evolves.

Timeline and Deliverables

To ensure that the IONA process is on track, prior to the end of each stage, the project manager should hold a review meeting at which the assessment team delivers a set of documents that consolidate the results of that stage's work and support the investigation in its next stage. The meeting should include a discussion about what the assessment has learned, challenges to the team's advancement to the next assessment stage, and how preparations for the next stage have progressed. Ideally, the project manager will advocate the sponsoring organization's interests and help the assessment team solve problems. The completion of each stage occurs when the project manager formally accepts all deliverables for that stage. At that point, the team moves to the next stage in the assessment process.

As a rule, the timeline for IONA encourages the assessment team to do as much work as possible prior to entering the field so that fieldwork consists primarily of testing and validating hypotheses developed during Stage 1. The timing and deliverables for each review meeting are suggested in table 6.

Because the project manager may make acceptance conditional on improvements to the deliverables, the review meetings must occur sufficiently in advance of the end of the stage to allow for corrections, particularly in Stage 1.[9] The timing of the review meeting in Stage 2 depends on the scope of the study and, consequently, how long the assessment team

Table 6. Review Meeting Timing and Deliverables for IONA Stages

	Stage 1 Defining the Assessment	Stage 2 Interviewing Informants	Stage 3 Designing Media Interventions
Review Meeting	2 weeks prior to departure for the field	7 to 10 days prior to returning from the field	2 weeks after returning from the field
Deliverables for passage to the next stage	► Scope of work ► Profile of media landscape and capabilities ► Preliminary list of issues, problems, and objectives ► Interview strategy ► Interview guides ► Interview roster	► Validated media profile ► Validated list of issues, problems, and needs ► Updated list of objectives ► List of completed interviews ► Expert list	► List of finalized objectives ► Preliminary list of interventions ► Outline for final report

expects to spend in the field. To allow the results of the review meeting to affect interviewing activity, the review meeting for Stage 2 should be scheduled no later than three-quarters of the time into Stage 2. The Stage 3 review does not have similar time constraints but should occur within two weeks after returning from the field so that the material is still fresh in the assessment team's minds. At minimum, the team should have completed the first two Stage 3 tasks (Finalize Intervention Objectives and Design Media Interventions) and sent the preliminary intervention designs to the expert panel as preparation for the Stage 3 review.

Conclusion

USIP's Intended-Outcomes Needs Assessment methodology guides assessment teams through the process of designing purposeful media interventions that have a high likelihood of success. The IONA three-stage assessment process enables the creation of a portfolio of media and non-media activities that effectively address the root causes of conflict.

USIP has developed a spreadsheet-based tool called IONA Frame Manager to support the IONA process. Native spreadsheet function enables the creation and management of an IONA database with rudimentary search, sort, ranking, filtering, and comparison functionality. This prototype will demonstrate proof-of-concept, allow estimates of a custom tool's effectiveness, and provide useful input to the custom tool's specification process. Researchers interested in using the spreadsheet should access USIP's Center for Media, Conflict and Peacebuilding Web site at http://www.usip.org/publications/iona to download a copy of this tool. Because it is in the prototype phase, users should contact USIP with ideas for improving the Frame Manager.

Using the insight developed from the spreadsheet-based prototype, USIP intendes to develop user-friendly custom software for IONA data management and analysis.

Framework for Profiling the Media Landscape

To use the media as a tool for social change, the assessment team must understand how the media operate in the target society. The following questions provide a framework for assessing the media landscape. During Stage 1 (Defining the Assessment) and early Stage 2 (Interviewing Respondents) of the assessment process, these questions allow the assessment team to identify the specific capabilities of the media in the target society.

In short, this profile determines how effective the media are as a tool for social change. If the media contribute to the fragility of the target society, the larger IONA assessment process will identify such issues and parts of the media will become targets for social change.

1. **Types of media**

    1.1 Print

    1.2 Radio

    1.3 Television

    1.4 Internet and other technologies

    1.5 Which of these media are:

    > 1.5.1 Community based (ethnicity, geography, language, etc.)?
    >
    > 1.5.2 Government run (overtly or covertly government run)?
    >
    > 1.5.3 Publicly owned?
    >
    > 1.5.4. Privately owned?

1.5.5 Religious?

1.5.6 Political?

2. Media consumers

2.1 Who reads which print media?

    2.1.1 Readership in terms of literacy rates

    2.1.2 Readership in terms of standard of living (cost of buying paper, magazines)

    2.1.3 Readership in terms of socioeconomic stratification (social class)

    2.1.4 Readership in terms of gender, ethnicity, religion, and other identity markers

    2.1.5 What is the reach of each print medium?

    2.1.6 Do readers trust the press?

2.2 Who listens to which radio networks?

    2.2.1 Overall penetration of radio

    2.2.2 Footprint of each broadcaster

    2.2.3 Audiences in terms of socioeconomic stratification (social class)

    2.2.4 Audiences in terms of gender, ethnicity, religion, and other identity markers

    2.2.5 Audiences in terms of language

    2.2.6 Do audiences trust radio broadcasts?

2.3 Who watches which TV networks?

    2.3.1 Overall penetration of TV

    2.3.2 Footprint of each broadcaster

    2.3.3 Viewers in terms of socioeconomic stratification (social class)

    2.3.4 Audiences in terms of gender, ethnicity, religion, and other identity markers

    2.3.5 Viewers in terms of language

    2.3.6 Do viewers trust TV broadcasts?

2.4   Who has Internet access?

    2.4.1   Overall penetration of Internet

    2.4.2   Availability

    2.4.3   Cost

    2.4.4   Internet use in terms of gender, ethnicity, religion, age, social class, and other identity markers

2.5   Who has a mobile phone?

    2.5.1   Overall penetration of cell phones

    2.5.2   Availability

    2.5.3   Cost

    2.5.4   Cell phone use in terms of gender, ethnicity, religion, social class, and other identity markers

    2.5.5   Do users believe/trust information coming via cell phones?

3.   Audiences served

3.1   Which social groups consume which media?

3.2   Which political groups consume which media?

3.3   Which identity groups consume which media?

3.4   How broadly is society reflected in which media?

3.5   Which of these media are

    3.5.1   Community based?

    3.5.2   User generated?

    3.5.3   Government run?

    3.5.4   Privately owned?

    3.5.5   Publicly owned?

    3.5.6   Religious?

    3.5.7   Political?

4.   Relationship between the media and minorities

4.1   Are minorities represented adequately in mainstream media? Do mainstream media misrepresent, under-represent, or fail to represent minorities?

4.2   Do minorities consume mainstream media?

4.3 Do minorities rely on or prefer

    4.3.1 Community-based or user-generated media?

    4.3.2 International media (native language broadcasts or foreign language)?

    4.3.3 Native-language media from a diaspora?

    4.3.4 Sources of information other than media?

4.4 Do minorities feel legitimized or demonized by mainstream media?

4.5 Does the majority feel legitimized or demonized by minority media?

5. Content

5.1 What kinds of programs are disseminated by which media, and by which formats?

5.2 Which programs are

    5.2.1 Local?

    5.2.2 National?

    5.2.3 Regional?

    5.2.4 Foreign/International?

5.3 Do media have content targeting particular audiences?

    5.3.1 Children

    5.3.2 Minorities (ethnic, religious, linguistic, etc.)

    5.3.3 Women

    5.3.4 Other specific target audiences

5.4 Do particular media promote specific

    5.4.1 Knowledge: which?

    5.4.2 Attitudes: which?

    5.4.3 Behaviors: which?

6. Access to media and information

6.1 How is information distributed or disseminated?

6.2 What technology systems exist?

6.3   What are the literacy levels?

6.4   What degree and kinds of censorship exist?

6.5   What language barriers exist?

6.6   What economic barriers (e.g., price of print media; need to pay radio/TV tax) exist?

7. **Ownership**

7.1   Who owns media?

7.2   Which media are owned by whom?

7.3   What is the ratio of government to private media?

7.4   How is media ownership regulated?

8. **Financing**

8.1   What media claim financial independence?

8.2   What is the relationship between a media outlet's finances and its editorial positions?

8.3   Are certain media financially advantaged (e.g., do they receive preferred advertising rates)?

8.4   How are media finances regulated?

9. **Level of professionalism**

9.1   Does a professional organization exist that monitors standards of behavior for the following media activities?

9.1.1   News media

9.1.2   Entertainment

9.1.3   Edutainment

9.2   How independent of political authority is this professional body?

9.3   How well defined are the standards defining the behavior of its members (e.g., editorial policies regarding impartiality, accuracy and objectivity, production values in media creation)?

9.4   How well does the professional organization monitor these standards and how does it enforce sanctions for misbehavior?

9.5   Who provides education and training for media practitioners?

9.5.1   Domestic/international organizations

9.5.2   Private/nongovernmental/governmental organizations

10. Media regulation

10.1   Which media regulations exist?

10.2   Do media practitioners know which regulations affect them?

10.3   Who creates and enforces media regulations?

10.4   Are media regulations created and enforced impartially and equitably?

10.5   Do professional associations or civil society groups monitor the media?

11. Relationship between the media and government

11.1   How do political entities (government, parties, or politicians) limit access by media to governmental information?

11.2   Are particular media channels owned by political entities?

11.2.1   How effectively do political entities use such media outlets to influence their target audiences?

11.2.2   Do such politicized media outlets generate conflict?

11.3   Do political entities restrict freedom of expression through legislation or other coercive means?

11.4   How do political entities punish media institutions or individuals who disobey?

11.5   To protect their political interests, do political entities co-opt managers, editors, and reporters in the media system?

11.5.1   How are media professionals selected for pressure?

11.5.2   How do political entities coerce media professionals?

Generic Interview Guide—
Validating and Ranking Issues

This interview guide is intended for use during Stage 2 to determine the most important issues confronting the target society or underpinning an issue that sponsors wish to address. The people scheduled for this type of interview must have broad rather than deep knowledge. Moreover, the interviewer must be careful not to allow the respondent to spend too much time on one particular topic. From the start, the interviewer should emphasize the comparative nature of the conversation and the need to develop an early understanding of the relative importance of different issues facing the target society.

Bring the most up-to-date list of high-importance issues (reflecting the results of the most recent interviews) and be sure to leave sufficient time to share the list with respondents and get their thoughts.

If respondents want to expand the list of the top issues to include more than three, they should be allowed. Finally, depending on the amount of time available, the interviewer should drill down into each issue area to understand what sub-issues are included.

		Question	Purpose
	1	► What are the top three most pressing issues facing your society? (Or, what are the top three most pressing issues concerning a problem identified by the sponsor as needing a media intervention?) Why? ► Are there particular issue areas within these three that are especially pressing? Why? ► Are these issues national or specific to one particular area? Why? ► Is there broad agreement on this? Would your political opponents give the same top three? Why?	To understand which issues are important to the target society. The number of issues investigated here depends on the scope of the assessment and the time allotted for the interview.
	2	► What are the top three most contentious issues facing your society? Which are among the leading causes of violent conflict? Why? ► If they weren't in answer to question 1, why weren't they?	To understand what issues cause dissension in the target society. The number of issues investigated here depends on the scope of the assessment and the time allotted for the interview.
	3	► Looking at this list of issues that we have identified as highly important, which three issues would you exclude as less pressing? Why? ► What would you replace them with?	To learn which issues are relatively less important. The number of issues investigated here depends on the scope of the assessment and the time allotted for the interview.

Issues Validation

Generic Interview Guide—
Contextualizing Issues of High
Importance

This interview guide is used during Stage 2 to determine where a society succeeded or failed to create change around an issue, and why. The interview begins by quickly getting a sense of which issues the respondent deems important. The assessment team should expect a reaffirmation of what they already know to be important. If the respondent's reply does not match the current list of high-importance issues, however, the interviewer should quickly probe to understand the discrepancy.

After using questions 1–3 to define the KAB that create the problem and delineate the need, the interviewer asks a series of questions intended to discover where on the Change Ladder the society sits with respect to this issue. With that knowledge, the interview shifts to discussing the successful transformations that brought the society to where it is and the failures it currently faces.

The interview team is responsible for framing these questions in terms that the respondent understands.

		Question	Purpose
Issues	0	▶ What are the top three issues facing your society? Why?	To continue refining what the team understands the top issues to be. To probe deeply on issues outside the current high-importance list.
Desired Change	1	▶ How does this issue manifest in current KAB held at some level in your society? ▶ How does this destabilize your society?	To understand the structure of KAB that defines the problem and the level at which the problem occurs.
	2	▶ What changes in KAB would improve your society? ▶ Why?	To understand the structure of KAB that defines what the respondent believes the society needs. This becomes the basis for defining an objective.
	3	▶ Why do you want this particular change? Why has it been difficult to realize?	To understand the benefits/ rewards and risk/sanctions the respondent attaches to this change.
Has Progress Occurred?	4a	▶ What approaches have been tried to implement alternatives to the status quo? ▶ Why have they not been successful?	Did progress end at Step 3 in the Change Ladder?
	4b	▶ If no alternatives have been tried, what approaches have promoted consideration of alternatives to the status quo? ▶ Why have they not been successful?	Did progress end at Step 2 in the Change Ladder?
	4c	▶ If no alternatives have been considered, what approaches have encouraged questioning of the status quo? ▶ Why have they not been successful?	Did progress end at Step 1 in the Change Ladder?

At this point, with respect to the issue being discussed, the interviewer understands the respondent's beliefs about his or her society's position on the Change Ladder. The goal for the rest of the interview is to understand why the society succeeded in getting to this point (if it is not Step 1 on the Change Ladder) and why there has been no further progress.

		Question	Purpose
Successful Change	5	▸ In trying to realize this desired change, what changes in KAB have successfully occurred? ▸ Which stakeholder groups were targeted at what level in society?	To understand what progress has occurred in addressing this issue. This question defines an objective for a successful change and the target group that had its KAB changed.
	6	▸ Who or what made that desired change possible? ▸ In what way did the benefits outweigh the risks?	To understand what facilitators and benefits support change in this issue.
	7	▸ Who or what opposed the desired change? ▸ How were they overcome? What convinced people to change?	To identify what obstacles opposed change and what was done to overcome that opposition.
	8	▸ What activities actually changed KAB? ▸ How was it learned?	To learn what activities facilitated a change in KAB. Could similar solutions activities work again?
Unsuccessful Change	9	▸ In trying to realize a desired change, what attempted changes in KAB have been unsuccessful? Why? ▸ Which stakeholder groups were targeted at what level in society?	To understand where progress has ended in addressing this issue. This question defines an objective for a successful change and the target group that refused to change its KAB.
	10	▸ Who or what supported this change? ▸ What was done to help them? Why did it fail?	To understand why the facilitators and benefits supporting change failed.
	11	▸ Who or what opposed the desired change? ▸ What was done to overcome their opposition? Why did it fail?	To identify what prevented the change and why it was not overcome.
	12	▸ What activities tried to change KAB? ▸ Why were the new KAB not adopted?	To learn what solutions activities (media or non-media) communicated, the information and opportunities that were to change objective KAB, and why those solutions activities failed.

Question	Purpose
The interviewer should investigate questions relating to unsuccessful change until there are no more unsuccessful attempts to report. The last two questions shift the discussion to new approaches, such as media not used or social change initiatives not yet attempted.	
13 ▸ Were there alternatives the society considered but didn't try?	To identify changes to KAB that were too far fetched, given the obstacles and risks facing actors in the target society.
14 ▸ What kind of media programs do you think could address the issues you've raised? Why have they not been tried? How effective would they be?	To identify media solutions activities that have not been tried.

The following pages show how these interview questions map on to the IONA frame.

Desired Change Frame

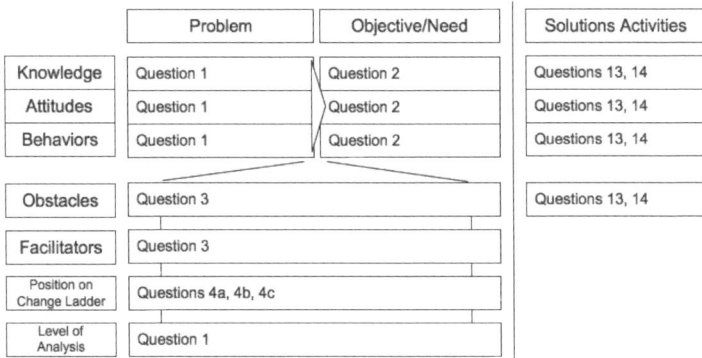

	Problem	Objective/Need	Solutions Activities
Knowledge	Question 1	Question 2	Questions 13, 14
Attitudes	Question 1	Question 2	Questions 13, 14
Behaviors	Question 1	Question 2	Questions 13, 14
Obstacles	Question 3		Questions 13, 14
Facilitators	Question 3		
Position on Change Ladder	Questions 4a, 4b, 4c		
Level of Analysis	Question 1		

Successful Change Frame

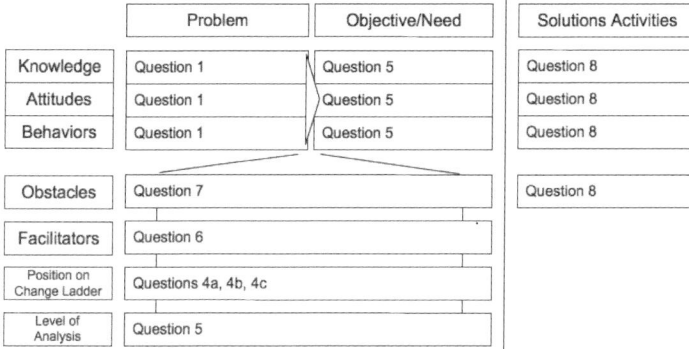

	Problem	Objective/Need		Solutions Activities
Knowledge	Question 1	Question 5		Question 8
Attitudes	Question 1	Question 5		Question 8
Behaviors	Question 1	Question 5		Question 8
Obstacles	Question 7			Question 8
Facilitators	Question 6			
Position on Change Ladder	Questions 4a, 4b, 4c			
Level of Analysis	Question 5			

Unsuccessful Change Frame

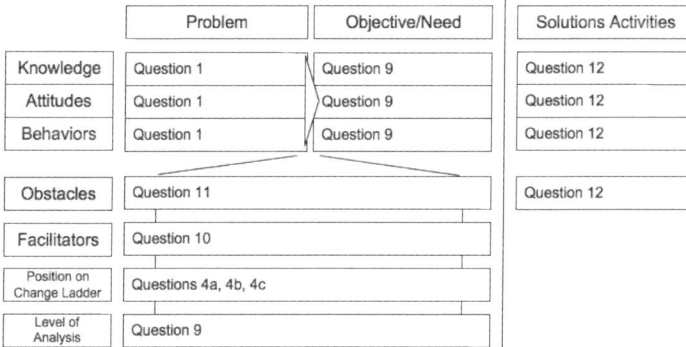

	Problem	Objective/Need		Solutions Activities
Knowledge	Question 1	Question 9		Question 12
Attitudes	Question 1	Question 9		Question 12
Behaviors	Question 1	Question 9		Question 12
Obstacles	Question 11			Question 12
Facilitators	Question 10			
Position on Change Ladder	Questions 4a, 4b, 4c			
Level of Analysis	Question 9			

Notes

1. Aaron Rhodes, *Ten Years of Media Support to the Balkan—An Assessment, Media Task Force of the Stability Challenges to Conventional Media Intervention Planning* (Amsterdam: Stability Pact for South East Europe and Press Now, 2007).

2. Craig LaMay, "Democratization and the Dilemmas of Media Independence," *International Journal of Not-for-Profit Law* 8, no. 4 (2006).

3. Shanthi Kalathil with John Langlois and Adam Kaplan, *Towards a New Model: Media and Communication in Post-Conflict and Fragile States* (Washington, D.C.: World Bank, 2008).

4. Gadi Wolfsfeld, "The News Media and Peace Processes: The Middle East and Northern Ireland," (Washington, D.C.: United States Institute of Peace, 2001).

5. Robert Karl Manoff, "The Media's Role in Preventing and Moderating Conflict," (presentation, United States Institute of Peace Virtual Media Conference, Washington, D.C., April 1–2, 1997).

6. Application of the KAB model in the healthcare field has enabled marked changes in social behavior in areas as different as reducing under-aged smoking and promoting safe sex practices among gay men. A large body of literature is available on communications for health-behavior change, especially regarding HIV/AIDS. Among the pertinent lessons learned is that this articulated process of change is applicable across cultures and geographic areas. AIDS interventions using the media have been conducted all over the world, including Africa, Southeast Asia, and the United States. For example, see Karoline Moon, "Knowledge, Perceptions, Attitudes, and Practices of HIV/AIDS: A Comparative Study of Behavior Change in Commercial Sex Workers and Truck Drivers in the Dindigul and Coimbatore Districts of Tamil Nadu, India," (master's thesis, Chapel Hill, North Carolina, 2002).

7. The authors wish to acknowledge Joseph Petraglia for his direct contribution to the development of our Change Ladder paradigm. Working on issues of health-related behavior change, Petraglia has created a method that he calls "pathways to change." See Joseph Petraglia, Christine Galavotti, Nicola Harford, Katina A. Pappas-DeLuca, and Maungo Mooki, "Applying Behavioral Science to Behavior Change Communication: The Pathways to Change Tools," *Health Promotion Practice* 8 (2007): 384–393.

8. For example, after fifty years of Communism (status quo), the populations of Poland, Hungary, Slovakia, and others had to consider a variety of political alternatives. They decided that their best choice was free-market capitalism, and voted accordingly. Ten years of capitalism (desired change), however, did not produce the benefits that were expected, especially economic benefits. The same voters, consequently, decided to return their former communist politicians to power, but under the rubric of Social Democrats (return to status quo).

9. Although it may be tempting to save airfare by buying tickets that have non-changeable departure dates, the review process is more effective if Stage 1 work is sufficiently advanced before the assessment team begins fieldwork. Flexibility about the departure date may be warranted.

About the Authors

Andrew Robertson is a leading innovator in using process modeling to design more efficient organizations. Drawing on a career of advising Fortune 500 corporations on functional best practice, he is applying these methods to improve the effectiveness of media and programming used to reduce conflict in fragile societies.

Eran Fraenkel is an expert and instructor in metrics and evaluation with more than 38 years of experience in international peacebuilding media. He is best known for his work on broadcast media, having produced numerous programs such as Naashe Maalo, an award-winning children's TV program on intercultural understanding and conflict prevention in Macedonia.

Sheldon Himelfarb directs the Center of Innovation for Media, Conflict and Peacebuilding. He has managed peacebuilding programs in numerous conflicts, including Bosnia, Iraq, Angola, Liberia, Macedonia, and Burundi. Himelfarb received the Capitol Area Peace Maker award from American University.

Emrys Schoemaker is a strategic and development communications specialist with particular expertise in leveraging new media for peacebuilding. He is an authority in designing and implementing national and local awareness and communication strategies and has worked with various government and United Nations agencies, as well as with international and local nongovernmental organizations throughout the Middle East.

About the United States Institute of Peace

The United States Institute of Peace is an independent, nonpartisan institution established and funded by Congress. The Institute provides analysis, training, and tools to help prevent, manage, and end violent international conflicts, promote stability, and professionalize the field of peacebuilding.

Chairman of the Board: J. Robinson West

Vice Chairman: George E. Moose

President: Richard H. Solomon

Executive Vice President: Tara Sonenshine

Chief Financial Officer: Michael Graham

.